Ears

Are for Earrings

THE SENSE OF HEARING

Katherine Hengel

Consulting Editor, Diane Craig, M.A./Reading Specialist

A Division of ABDO

ABDO
Publishing Company

visit us at www.abdopublishing.com

Published by ABDO Publishing Company, a division of ABDO, P.O. Box 398166, Minneapolis, Minnesota 55439. Copyright © 2012 by Abdo Consulting Group, Inc. International copyrights reserved in all countries. No part of this book may be reproduced in any form without written permission from the publisher. SandCastle™ is a trademark and logo of ABDO Publishing Company.

Printed in the United States of America, North Mankato, Minnesota
102011
012012

 PRINTED ON RECYCLED PAPER

Editor: Liz Salzmann
Content Developer: Nancy Tuminelly
Cover and Interior Design and Production: Oona Gaarder-Juntti, Mighty Media, Inc.
Photo Credits: BananaStock, Digital Vision, Jack Hollingsworth, Jupiterimages, Medioimages, Photodisc, Shutterstock, Thinkstock

Library of Congress Cataloging-in-Publication Data
Hengel, Katherine.
 Ears are for earrings : the sense of hearing / Katherine Hengel.
   p. cm. -- (All about your senses)
 ISBN 978-1-61783-196-6
 1. Ear--Juvenile literature. 2. Senses and sensation--Juvenile literature. I. Title.
 QP462.2.H46 2012
 612.8'5--dc23
                              2011023462

SandCastle™ Level: Transitional

SandCastle™ books are created by a team of professional educators, reading specialists, and content developers around five essential components—phonemic awareness, phonics, vocabulary, text comprehension, and fluency—to assist young readers as they develop reading skills and strategies and increase their general knowledge. All books are written, reviewed, and leveled for guided reading, early reading intervention, and Accelerated Reader® programs for use in shared, guided, and independent reading and writing activities to support a balanced approach to literacy instruction. The SandCastle™ series has four levels that correspond to early literacy development. The levels are provided to help teachers and parents select appropriate books for young readers.

| Emerging Readers | Beginning Readers | Transitional Readers | Fluent Readers |
| (no flags) | (1 flag) | (2 flags) | (3 flags) |

Table of Contents

Ears

Are for Earrings

Denise got her ears **pierced**!
Her first earrings were small.
Now she can wear bigger ones!

What else are ears for? What
can ears sense?

Ears

Are for Hearing

Amy is running in a race. She waits to hear the starting **whistle**. She got third place last time. She wants first place this time!

Our ears pick up sounds. Then our brains figure out what the sounds mean. That's how we hear!

Our Sense of
Hearing

Our ears help us sense the world around us. Sensing with our ears is called hearing. Hearing is one of our five senses.

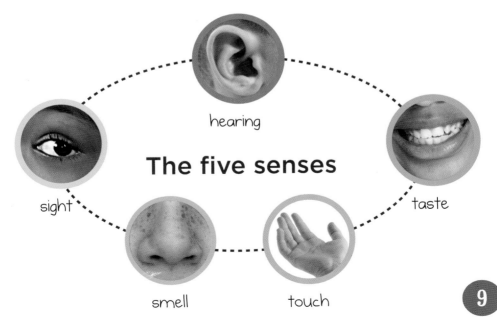

hearing

The five senses

sight

taste

smell

touch

Ears

Hear Quiet Sounds

Phil hears his teacher. She is talking softly. Other students are working. She doesn't want to **disturb** them.

Ears
Hear Loud Sounds

Sara yells into a **megaphone**. She is cheering for the football team. Her **cousin** is the quarterback!

Ears hear a lot!
What else can ears do?

Ears

Are for Secrets

Adam tells Justin a secret.
It's about a birthday present!
Adam whispers so no one
else can hear.

Ears

Are for Plugging

We cover our ears when we don't want to hear. Peggy's brother is practicing the drums. Peggy doesn't like the way it sounds!

Ears

Are for Headphones

Roger listens to music with his headphones. He bought some new songs. He's already listened to them three times!

Ears

Can Hear and Do a Lot!

Billy is glad that his ears can hear so well. He enjoys listening to the many different sounds that he hears every day.

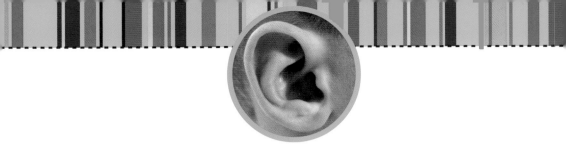

Facts About Hearing

◆ You can't turn off your ears. Not even when you are asleep!

◆ Snakes cannot hear. They do not have ears.

◆ Kids hear more than adults! Kids can recognize a wider **variety** of sounds.

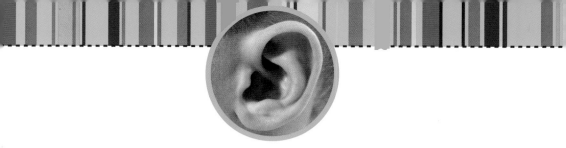

Hearing Quiz

1. Our brains figure out what sounds mean. True or false?

2. Hearing is one of the five senses. True or false?

3. Ears cannot hear quiet sounds. True or false?

4. Roger only listened to his new songs one time. True or false?

Answers 1. True 2. True 3. False 4. False

Glossary

cousin – a child of your aunt or uncle.

disturb – to bother or interrupt.

megaphone – a device shaped like a cone that is used to make the voice louder.

pierce – to poke a hole through something.

variety – different types of one thing.

whistle – a loud, high sound.